Far from Sodom
Вдали от Содома

Inna Lisnianskaya

Far from Sodom

Вдали от Содома

Translated by Daniel Weissbort
Introduced by Elaine Feinstein

PUBLICATIONS
2005

Published by Arc Publications,
Nanholme Mill, Shaw Wood Road
Todmorden OL14 6DA, UK

Copyright © Inna Lisnianskaya 2005
Translation copyright © Daniel Weissbort 2005
Introduction copyright © Elaine Feinstein 2005

Design by Tony Ward
Printed by Antony Rowe Ltd
Eastbourne, East Sussex

ISBN 1 904614 14 0

ACKNOWLEDGEMENTS

This selection of Inna Lisnianskaya's poetry is taken from two
collections. A distinction is made in Russian between a regular
poem, *stikhi* or *stikhotvorenie*, and a poem usually of large
proportions, *poema*.

Odinokii dar: Stikhi; Poemy [Lonely gift: Poems, Long po-
ems], O.G..I., Moscow, 2003

Bez tebia [Without you]. Russkii put', Moscow, 2004.

The title of the present collection, *Far from Sodom*, is a free
translation of the title of one of Inna Lisnianskaya's recent
collections in Russian, *V prigorode Sodoma*, O.G.I., Moscow,
2002 (see the biographical note on Inna Lisnianskaya).

The publishers acknowledge financial assistance
from ACE Yorkshire

**Arc Publications: 'Visible Poets' series
Editor: Jean Boase-Beier**

For
Semyon Izrailevich Lipkin

Contents

Contents

Series Editor's Note

There is a prevailing view of translated poetry, especially in England, which maintains that it should read as though it had originally been written in English. The books in the 'Visible Poets' series aim to challenge that view. They assume that the reader of poetry is by definition someone who wants to experience the strange, the unusual, the new, the foreign, someone who delights in the stretching and distortion of language which makes any poetry, translated or not, alive and distinctive. The translators of the poets in this series aim not to hide but to reveal the original, to make it visible and, in so doing, to render visible the translator's task too. The reader is invited not only to experience the unique fusion of the creative talents of poet and translator embodied in the English poems in these collections, but also to speculate on the processes of their creation and so to gain a deeper understanding and enjoyment of both original and translated poems.

Jean Boase-Beier

Translator's Preface

It is surely axiomatic that one should translate only that to which one is drawn. So, it is appropriate to ask myself: what drew me to Lisnianskaya's poetry? There is a danger, of course – if one may speak of dangers – that, in being drawn to something, one is likely to want to "make it one's own", that is, to try to *remake* it. But herein lies a paradox, since, without that initial pull of the familiar "other", there is no beginning.

In the first place, I was surprised that Lisnianskaya, who has been a feature of the Russian poetry scene for so long, should have escaped my notice until I came across her name when my wife Valentina Polukhina was researching Russian women poets for a special issue of *Modern Poetry in Translation* (No. 20, 2002) which she and I co-edited. I "assigned" Lisnianskaya to Ruth Fainlight, who produced several fine translations on the basis of literal versions with which my wife and I provided her. More poems by Lisnianskaya are also to be found in *In the Grip of Strange Thoughts: Russian Poetry in a New Era*, edited by J. Kates (Zephyr, 1990) translated by Judith Hemschemeyer who has also edited and translated, for the same publisher, *The Complete Poems of Anna Akhmatova*. Hemschemeyer's interest in Lisnianskaya is not surprising, since if there is one predecessor to whom this poet bears a resemblance it is to Akhmatova. The late Nobel laureate Joseph Brodsky, for instance, wrote of her (*Russkaya Mysl,* 3 February 1983):

> Of what I have read in the last few years, Lisnianskaya's poems have impressed me most. Russian poets, poets in general, are the product of what has been written before. They start by alluding to or contradicting it. The only echo I clearly discern in Lisnianskaya's poetry is that of Akhmatova […].

That is a view from within, although in actual fact Brodsky was located abroad. I myself am reminded of what Ted Hughes wrote of another English poet, his Cambridge contemporary Daniel Huws, in a blurb to Huws's first poetry collection *Noth* (1972). He alludes to "the all-inclusive wholly human wholly musical final simplicity of the oldest folk-rhymes and songs." I find a similar quality of folk pithiness, of engagement in Lisnianskaya's poetry. Of course, as far as the music goes, translation can at best substitute, and substitution of one music, the translator's, for another, the unrepeatable music of the source text, may be seen as a perilous stratagem. What interests me about this comment by Hughes is the notion of a "final simplicity" pertaining to "folk-rhymes and songs". As a non-Russian I cannot fully gauge the extent to which Lisnianskaya draws on or is drawn to such traditional material; but I can sense a finality in her "wholly human" lines and stanzas that relates to an archetypal substratum. Of course, in so characterising it, I am opening myself, to say the least, to the scepticism of critics, still reacting to the vagueness, the wishful thinking of Romanticism.

Almost half a century ago now, I found myself drawn – for historical and personal reasons – to the poetry of the first post-World War Two generation of Eastern European poets. In my youthful enthusiasm or tactlessness I tended to contrast what I found in their work with what seemed lacking in homegrown products. I was impressed by a commitment to human dignity, an awareness of the direness of the threat not only to that dignity, but to the very survival of our species, an ability to confront human suffering, the violence, cruelty that typified our era. At the same time, there was an unadorned quality about the language that made it – or seemed to make it – eminently translatable. Translatability even became a kind of test of quality, almost a guarantee of authenticity. It was as though the roots of a universal language were being recovered or uncovered. In a predictable, if surprisingly long delayed reaction to this, it has now become quite fashionable – on both sides of the former Iron Curtain – to decry the so-called "Eastern European Poem", which is felt by some critics to be readily imitable or reductive. (This reaction is in part, one supposes, the consequence of competition between the generations.)

Translatability, in some cases, seemed to relate to a songlike quality which paradoxically transcended language, a lyricism attaching itself to meaning, the means, rather than to the actual texture of the language. It is this particular songlike quality that I find again in Lisnianskaya, who belongs to the same post-war generation. She seems to me constitutionally incapable, as it were, of dishonesty or subterfuge; what is translatable can ultimately and hardly surprisingly be identified with what is human, and it is its humanness that typifies her work.

It is surely not necessary to rehearse, in a series like this, one's dissatisfaction, as a translator, with the results of one's work, to comment in detail on what, for instance, has been "lost" in the process. Inevitably, it seems to me, translation dissolves the original unity of form and content, which characterizes any poetry of substance and quality. What has been lost is obvious enough to those familiar with the source-language texts. Thus, there is, in Lisnianskaya's poetry, a vibrancy that recalls that of Marina Tsvetaeva. Russian women poets almost inevitably must negotiate between Tsvetaeva and Akhmatova; revealingly, Lisnianskaya, in an interview with Tatyana Vaizer (*Literaturnaya Gazeta*, April 2000), says of her great predecessor: "Akhmatova borrowed her music not from Kuzmin, as was long claimed, but from Tsvetaeva. [...] The music of words is not music as we understand it. Even poets who don't have a musical ear can create a music of words, as a doctor can hear missing beats in the heart's rhythm." This "music" is evident in an abruptness that often underlies and sometimes seems to contradict the classical serenity of the form. I doubt whether it can be reinvented in English without compromising the translation, without, that is, distancing the reader to such an extent that contact with the source text is jeopardized. At best, I would contend – many Russian poets would disagree – it can only be suggested in translation. And yet, it is surely the translator's duty to remain aware of it at all times; he or she must be prepared to tolerate the anguish of being unable to reproduce what must be taken as an *essential* aspect of the source texts! In this (to say the least) uncomfortable but endlessly challenging situation, I find myself opting for a kind of pragmatism rather than aspiring to consistency. That is, I am reconciled to taking advantage of such opportunities as present themselves, while (I hope) keeping the integrity of the poem in view. Unfortunately, one can hardly give examples of one's supposed successes in this respect without seeming to be bullying the reader into underwriting one's decisions or compromises.

I prefer to dwell for a few moments on what may be *gained* in translating a poet like Lisnianskaya, also on what may be preserved. Of course, I believe that much can be preserved, or I'd not be undertaking the task at all! One aspect, for instance, of her work which does yield somewhat to translation is its descriptive precision or energy. As Anna Akhmatova focused with exactitude on time and place, as well as feeling, so Lisnianskaya focuses on appearance, by which I do not mean the superficial. But, while her work, metaphysically and metaphorically, is highly sophisticated, she is also a poet of instinct, for whom the outer shape of things mirrors the inner reality, the emotional force. She exemplifies a particular poetic virtue, that of allowing the poem to speak for itself, with minimal intervention or commentary. This characteristic is, of course, typical, if one may say so, of the lyric gift, which is why – as Brodsky notes – it is by her short lyrics that Lisnianskaya is best represented.

I hope that the present selection of her poetry will serve to introduce a poet, the brevity of whose utterances belies the universal, the truly tragic nature of her vision.

Daniel Weissbort, 2005

14

Introduction

Inna Lisnianskaya's poems have a quiet music: there is no fizz of metaphor, no effort to draw attention to the language in which they are written; all her energy goes into a lucid honesty. She belongs with George Herbert rather than John Donne. In a Russian context, her conversational tone recalls Anna Akhmatova rather than Marina Tsvetaeva. Yet whatever echoes admirers identify in her voice, Lisnianskaya is a true original. She chooses subjects without glamour and infuses them with passionate emotions not commonly acknowledged. It is a long while since I have been so excited by the discovery of a new poet.

Lisnianskaya was born in Baku in 1928. Though she has by now been awarded the State Prize and the Solzhenitsyn Prize, and has been writing for four decades, I have the impression such recognition came late. Yet it is possible to believe her when she shrugs off questions in a recent interview in *Literaturnaya Gazeta* with a laconic: "I have had my say." The interviewer watches her sitting with a cigarette between long fingers and draws a comparison between her presence and Anna Akhmatova in the famous aquamarine and yellow portrait painted by Natan Altman. Lisnianskaya is not flattered. "I'm comfortable enough with myself," she says in the same interview. "I was never particularly loved by anyone."

There is not the least self-pity in her voice, and several of her poems have the same casual matter-of-factness:

I don't consider myself one of the unfortunate,
My life suits me well...

Yet the need for love is one of her key themes. In an early poem, she begins with a woman who slips out of her clothes, observing her own dress, with something like compassion, because it hangs like a prison smock:

"Enough of loneliness!"
Thought I in despair,
At dusk slipping off my dress
As a snake sloughs its skin.

At the end of the poem, we discover "a stranger's cheek / Sleep-

15

ily brushed mine." He is lying in her bed: a whole story has been collapsed into one short lyric.

In the same *Literaturnaya Gazeta* interview, she was asked whether she did not think that she might yet have her best poetry still to write. She ridiculed the idea: "At my age?" Yet it is her recent poems that are most memorable. She writes fearlessly about the love between men and women whose bodies have aged. She and her late husband, the celebrated poet Semyon Lipkin, moved to the writer's village of Peredelkino just outside Moscow not long before he died. Their love for one another colours many of her poems without the least sentimentality. One of my favourite lyrics in this selection is "Jealousy", which has nothing to do with sexual possessiveness, still less female anxiety; instead describes with affectionate mockery how a husband cannot bear other people to share the attention he wants from his wife. It is an analysis of some subtlety. The story opens before the poem starts, perhaps with the man leaving their apartment in a temper:

I look out the window at the retreating back.
Your jealousy is both touching and comical.
Can't you see I am old and scary, a witch,
And apart from you no-one needs me at all!

She reflects it is at once touching and funny that he wants to send everyone who comes to visit them packing, even though they have brought flowers and are glad to know she is nursing him. More deeply, she sees their visitors' emotions are ambivalent, and recognises they may observe the close interplay of husband and wife with their own jealousies:

And my attachment, the truth of my love, no less,
They envy. So, keep your jealousy buttoned up!
In this world, with its surfeit of painful loss,
Let me open the door with a smile on my lips.

Both she and Lipkin are Jewish, and this gives her poems a complex resonance. She remembers her father, an army doctor who was wounded and decorated in the Second World War, dreaming of gas ovens. In a poem written in 1975, when it was impossible to travel to Israel from the Soviet Union without becoming a "refuznik", she wishes him a fiddler to "play Israel's lament" for him, since she doubts whether he will ever reach his "Forbidden Land".

After the collapse of Communism, when she and her husband are able to visit Jerusalem, they pause at the Jaffa Gate. The poem that she makes from the experience is deeply moving, and for all its pitiless scrutiny of aging flesh, has a wry humour:

> I'm your Shulamith, my old King Solomon,
> Your muscles are slack, but your sight still sharp.
> Nothing's withheld from you, but peering at the slope,
> You do not recognize me, draped from head to foot
> Among the old women gathering grapes.

She confesses ruefully that he would know her no better if she were naked, even if she revealed her "belly / like undulant sands, legs stiff, unlike the vine / My breast, the withered fruit of an ancient palm." Fortunately, their love for one another had always been fed by an exchange of songs – she remembers particularly the loving words he found to compare her hair to flashing sunlight – and so even in old age she can rejoice in him:

> I inhaled your speech, as a bee inhales pollen,
> My king, Solomon, your love-hymn to beauty.

On 8 November 2003, a poem ("I look down from the mountain, the fourth floor") which must recall this trip to Israel, brings images of date-palms, eucalyptus and camels, into a description of a Moscow landscape. The true subject of the poem is an oldfashioned block of flats, heavily charged with memories. What she remembers is:

> ... the creaking Moscow elevator
> We went in alone, and kissed

The poem, written after the recent death of her husband, concludes without the least attempt to distance emotion:

> ... This scape
> Receives the pine coffin, as a car slides into a garage.
> Your death is the reality; my life a mirage.

It is in her poems about death – always a key theme for a lyric poet, as Brodsky points out – that she is closest to the English seventeenth century:

> Do not cremate me after life –
> Let the worm have his fill, the raspberry canes enjoy.

She is able to move from the casual spirit of that opening to a conclusion which hits hard without magniloquence:

> There are no raspberries in the graveyard, only
> My dear ones. No sandy pall.
> After death? It's not about me,
> But the one who did not die at all.

Quirky, surprising, often amused, her stance is never ingratiating:

> I noticed, everybody got
> Tired of me, happy or not.

She writes without evident distress, and concludes

> And, perhaps, when I am through,
> My grave will weary of me too.

Lisnianskaya's lyricism, as her translator Daniel Weissbort puts it, seems *to transcend language*; that is, hers is a lyricism of meaning and feeling so intense that it renders language seemingly transparent. She writes with a precision and immediacy to which we can respond even though the texture of the Russian language is necessarily absent. Weissbort's own translations are clean, clear and sometimes amazingly felicitous, as in the last verse of this late poem:

> Only the wind brings happiness,
> Like the smell of freshly baked bread.
> The wind does not know what has happened,
> And is not dismayed by what's ahead.

Elaine Feinstein, 2005

Far from Sodom
Вдали от Содома

Забвенья нету сладкого…

Забвенья нету сладкого,
Лишь горькое в груди, –
Защиты жди от слабого,
От сильного не жди.

Такое время адово
На нынешней Руси –
Проси не у богатого,
У бедного проси.

Наглядны все прозрения,
Все истины просты, –
Не у святых прощения,
У грешников проси.

[1967]

No sweet oblivion…

No sweet oblivion,
Only rancour in the breast,
For protection look to the weak,
Not the strong.

Poisonous times
In this, our Russia.
Don't ask the rich for alms –
The poor.

All prophesies, all truths
Are plain.
Ask forgiveness of sinners,
Not saints.

[1967]

Платье

«С меня одиночества хватит!» –
Отчаявшись, думала я,
Снимая при сумерках платье,
Как кожу снимает змея.

…На улице вяло светало –
Мешало обилье дождя, –
Беспомощно платье свисало
Со вбитого в стенку гвоздя.

В нём было такое безволье,
Такое – совсем ничего,
Что было мне жалко до боли
Совсем не себя, а его.

Оно мне казнённым казалось,
Когда в полутёмном дому
Чужое лицо прикасалось
Дремотно к лицу моему.

[1968]

The dress

"Enough of loneliness!"
Thought I in despair,
At dusk slipping off my dress
As a snake sloughs its skin.

Outside the light was dim,
In the window a rainy squall –
The dress hung there limp
From a nail banged into the wall.

It was so weak-willed,
So utterly null,
I felt pity for it,
For myself, none.

It looked like a prison smock,
In the half-dark house when
A stranger's cheek
Sleepily brushed mine.

[1968]

А вспомним ли мы…

М. Петровых

А вспомним ли мы
Через несколько лет,
Что был у зимы
Мелодический свет,

Что ловит земля
Сквозь метели и льды
Стеклянное «ля»
Вифлеемской звезды.

А вспомнит ли нас
Через несколько лет
В серебряный час
Колокольный рассвет?

[1972]

Will we recall...

To M. Petrovykh

Will we recall
A few years hence
That winter's light
Was melodious,

That the earth can hear
The glassy "lah",
Through sleet and snow,
Of Bethlehem's star?

And in a few years
Will we recall
In a silvery hour
The peel of dawn?

[1972]

Ахматовой

Сюда, где забвенье с изменою
И с совестью путают срам,
Приходит Простая, Надменная
И будит меня по утрам.

И я пристаю к ней с вопросами:
Куда и зачем нам идти,
Зачем раскалёнными розами
Мы хлещем себя по груди?

Ведь это – не женский заведомо,
К тому же шиитский обряд.
Зачем же от слова заветного
Вседневно ожоги горят?

[1973]

Цветаевой

Легка твоя посмертная кровать,
У смерти времени не занимать,
Здесь есть досуг над жизнью поразмыслить:
Родится гений, чтоб ничтожного возвысить,
Ничтожный – чтобы гения попрать.

[1974]

To Akhmatova

Where oblivion and betrayal,
Like conscience and shame,
Merge – Haughty and Simple,
She rouses me each day.

I ply her with questions
Where and why should we go?
Why do we beat our breasts
With roses that scald?

This is not wittingly female,
No Muslim rite, I say!
Why does the sacred word
Scald us each day?

[1973]

To Tsvetaeva

Your posthumous couch is weightless,
Death yields no extra time to us.
But to muse, there's still sufficient:
A genius is born to raise the insignificant,
Insignificance, to confound the genius.

[1974]

27

Там цвели вдоль моря олеандры…

Там цвели вдоль моря олеандры,
Розовая тень ушла в песок,
Ударяли голосом Кассандры
Волны в парапет наискосок.
Не она ли грозно прорицала,
Что взойдёт кровавая звезда
И на север тронутся с вокзала
Зарешеченные поезда,
Что в одном из них уйдёт в потемки,
В шахту, в мерзлоту, за Енисей
Инженер по нефтеперегонке –
Дядя твой, курчавый Елисей,
И что брат от брата отречётся:
С проработки твой отец вернётся,
Повернёт в двух скважинах ключи, –
И альбом семейный захлебнётся
Керосином в кафельной печи,
Что бутылку из-под керосина
Бабушка к груди своей прижмет,
Как бы убаюкивая сына,
И протяжно-влажно запоёт…

[1976]

Lining the seashore, oleanders…

Lining the seashore, oleanders,
Blending with the sand, the red and white,
And waves with the voice of Cassandra
Striking the parapet sideways on.
Wasn't it she so grimly told
How a bloody star would rise
And the prison trains would roll
Northwards from the terminus,
That curly-headed Elias.
Your uncle, an oil engineer,
Would penetrate that murk, the permafrost,
The mines beyond the Yelisei,
That brothers would deny each other,
And your father, back from the hearing,
Would turn the key twice in the lock,
And in the tiled stove the family album
Would choke on kerosene, and grandma
With a long lament or lullaby,
Would rock the empty bottle,
As if it were her baby boy.

[1976]

Мой отец – военный врач…

Мой отец – военный врач,
Грудь изранена.
Но играй ему, скрипач,
Плач Израиля!
Он за музыку, как пульс,
Нитевидную,
Отдал пенсию, клянусь,
Инвалидную.
Он, как видишь, не ловкач –
Орден к ордену,
Но играй ему, скрипач,
Не про родину.
Бредит он вторую ночь
Печью газовой,
– Не пишись еврейкой, дочь,
Мне наказывал.
Ах, играй, скрипач, играй!
За победою
Пусть ему приснится край
Заповеданный!
За него ль он отдал жизнь
Злую, милую?
Доиграй и помолись
Над могилою.

[1975]

My father was an army doctor...

My father was an army doctor,
Wounds, he'd plenty of,
But play to him, fiddler, play
Israel's lament.
He gave his veteran's pension for
This thin, throbbing wail,
No malingerer was he –
Medal upon medal.
Still, fiddler, do not play
Songs of the motherland.
For two nights he's been dreaming of
The gas ovens.
"Listen, daughter," he urged,
"Don't write Jew."
Play to him, ah, play!
After the victory,
May he dream
Of the forbidden land!
Did he give his precious
Angry life for that?
And, the playing done, pray
By his graveside.

[1975]

Рукой слезу останови…

Рукой слезу останови,
Не бойся горестного знанья –
Проходит время для любви,
Приходит для воспоминанья.

И возникают острова
Твоей любви, твоей Эллады,
И повторяются слова
Твоей тоски, твоей услады, –

И ты ни с кем уже не врозь,
И нет разлуки за свиданьем,
И даже то, что не сбылось,
Становится воспоминаньем.

[1980]

Brush away a tear...

Brush away a tear,
Do not fear the grievous knowledge –
The time for loving has passed,
The time for memory nears.

And islands of your love,
Your Hellas, rise up,
And your words of joy
And of longing are repeated.

And already there's no parting
For you, no hail and farewell,
Afterwards, even that
Which never was, a memory.

[1980]

Кошка

Где кошка твоя, гуляющая
        Сама по себе,
Молочный туман лакающая
        В густом сентябре?

Где поступь её леопардовая
        И фосфор во мгле,
Где кошка твоя и где правда твоя
        На этой земле?

Где кошка, ещё не отловленная,
        Где крыша и течь?
Где скоростью звука надломленная
        Охриплая речь?

Где осень твоя ясновидческая
        И снов закрома?
Где кошка твоя фосфорическая
        И где ты сама?

[1983]

Cat

Where is your cat, walking
    On its own,
Lapping the milky mist
    Amid September?

Where its leopard tread,
    Its phosphorescence,
Where is your cat and your truth
    Where on this earth?

Where is the cat, still not found,
    Where the roof and the leak in it?
Where is the hoarse speech
    Broken by the speed of sound?

Where is your clairvoyant autumn
    And corn-bins of dreams?
Where is your phosphorescent cat
    And you yourself?

[1983]

Видишь, сама я себе западня…

Видишь, сама я себе западня:
Людям кричу среди белого дня, –
Вот она я – унижайте меня!
Вот она я – распинайте меня!

Чёрного крику мне хватит на три
Не петушиных – вороньих зари.
Будут не в колокола звонари
Бить, а в сияющие фонари.

Я, заклеймённая жгучей виной,
Я, в ожиданье расправы со мной,
Буду толочь под кирпичной стеной
Стёкла фонарные голой ступнёй.

Боже, о чём я Тебе говорю?
Это в бреду я три ночи горю,
Колокола раскачали зарю...
Боже, о чём я Тебе говорю?

[1983]

I am a trap to myself, don't you see...

I am a trap to myself, don't you see:
In full daylight, I suddenly scream:
Here I am! Humiliate me!
Here I am! Crucify me!

My black outcry is good for three dawns,
No rooster's howl, but a raven's caw.
The bell-ringers will toll
Not the bells, but glowing lamps.

Branded by guilt, I
Await retribution from on high.
The glass of the lamp I shall crush
By the brick wall, under my bare foot.

Lord, oh, what am I saying to You?
Three fevered nights, crazed, forlorn,
The bells have shaken loose the dawn.
Lord, what am I saying to you?

[1983]

День пылает над рощей редеющей…

День пылает над рощей редеющей,
Всё живое к реке накреня,
А в груди моей угль холодеющий,
Обжигающий только меня.

Мне ль перечить пространству огромному,
Не познавшему душу свою?
Мне ль чужой быть скоту подъярёмному,
В чьём сословье и я состою?

Много ль надо мне? Хлеба обдирного
Да воды, и забыть, что вода
Мне остатком потопа всемирного
Почему-то казалась всегда.

Много ль надо? Но знаю заранее,
Что сама я пойду на убой,
Что сама я пойду на заклание
Водопойной наклонной тропой.

[1983]

Day flares above the thinning grove…

Day flares above the thinning grove,
Tilts all that lives towards the stream,
And in my breast a coal grows cold,
Scalding me alone.

Should I confront the great expanse,
Which does not know its own soul?
Should I from the beasts of burden distance
Myself, although I am one of that herd?

What do I need? A little bread,
Water, and to forget
That for some reason it always seemed
Left over from the Flood.

What do I need? I know before
To take myself to the place of slaughter,
Down the track to the gully,
To be sacrificed.

[1983]

Мы люди, мы прописаны в Гоморре...

Мы люди, мы прописаны в Гоморре
И не испепеляемся в огне.
Шумит, как грех неискуплённый, море,
Но иногда я слышу в полусне –

Рыдает сам Господь за облаками
Рыданием разгневанной любви:
Вы – ангелы мои, но оболгали
Самих себя и сделались людьми.

[1988]

We people are entered under Gomorrah…

We people are entered under Gomorrah –
Not to be reduced to ash by the fire.
The sea rages, like unexpiated sin,
But at times, half asleep, I hear

The Lord Himself sobbing behind the clouds
With a sob of outraged love:
You are my angels but have become
As men, by yourselves traduced.

[1988]

Дождь в январе

О чём ты, дождь, о чём, печальник?
Да и пора твоя прошла.
Опять курю, пододеяльник
Опять, задумавшись, прожгла.

О том ли плачешь, что охота
Вернуться в глушь опальных дней,
Где я провидческую ноту
Брала на скрипочке твоей,

Не мне ли вторишь, что воспитан
Живить долины и холмы,
А нынче ядами пропитан,
Которые извергли мы?

О чём ты, дождь, о чём, рыдальник?
Иль вправду мир наш проморгал,
Что он стоит как подзеркальник
Без трёх магических зеркал?

[1989]

The rain in January

What's the matter, rain?
Sad one, your time is over.
I'm smoking again, and again,
I've burned the cover!

Do you weep because you want
To take yourself off in disgrace,
To where I struck a prophetic note
On your trickle of strings,

Going on about how you were raised
To keep hill and valley lit,
And now are saturated
With the poisons we excreted?

What's the matter, cry-baby,
Did you really miss our
World, like a dressing-table
Minus those three magic mirrors?

[1989]

Ночь на Рождество

Кто говорит, что мы должны страдать,
Уязвлены терновою занозой,
Когда звезда умеет так сиять
И пахнуть осликом и розой.

Кто дарит блеск рассветного луча
Звезде, напоминающей о розе, –
И ночь тепла, как с царского плеча
Соболья шуба на морозе.

Что нужно яслям прежде и потом? –
Избыток сердца и остаток сенца.
Мы связаны друг с другом не крестом,
А пуповиною Младенца.

[1993]

Christmas Eve

Who's to say it is our lot
To suffer the thorn's abuse,
When the star can shine so bright
And smell of donkey and rose.

Who is it, at dawn,
Infuses the roselike star with light,
And the night, like sable, warm
On the Tsar's shoulder, in the frost.

What's the manger's need before and after?
Heart and hay to spare. It's not
The cross joins one to the other,
But the Infant's umbilical cord.

[1993]

Я сама себе колыбельную…

Я сама себе колыбельную
Каждый вечер пою:
Спи, скиталица, пыль метельную
Не увидишь в раю!

Сделал походя твой возлюбленный
Из голубки змею,
Спи, бесстыдница, взгляд потупленный
Ты не встретишь в раю!

В ночь безлюдную, новогоднюю
Дунь на свечку свою:
Спи, безумица, преисподнюю
Ты не вспомнишь в раю!

[1990]

Each night, I lullaby…

Each night, I lullaby
Myself. Wanderer, sleep,
You'll not see the whirling dust
Bestrewing paradise.

Your beloved casually
Out of a dove made a snake.
Sleep, shameless one, you'll not see
In paradise a bashful gaze.

In solitude, at night, blow
On your New Year's candle;
Sleep, crazy one, in paradise
You'll not recall the nether realm.

[1990]

Июльский холст

Стезя моя проста,
При мне моё искомое, –
Знакомые места,
Как музыка знакомая.

Да и мечта проста, –
Я грежу лишь о сбывшемся, –
О вязе у моста
И доме облупившемся.

И пища в нём проста, –
С соседских грядок овощи
И ягоды с куста –
Без посторонней помощи.

И смерть моя проста, –
Призналась, что ей велено
Стереть меня с холста,
Где розово и зелено.

[1990]

July canvas

My path is plain,
I have what I seek,
Familiar places,
Like familiar music.

And my dream is plain:
What has come to pass, –
The elm-tree by the bridge,
The peeling house.

And the food there is plain –
From neighbouring plots, vegetables
And berries from a bush,
Gathered with no outside help.

And my death, too, is plain,
Acknowledging it has been told
To erase me from the canvas,
Where there is green and rose.

[1990]

У тайны нет загадочной повадки…

У тайны нет загадочной повадки,
Она проста, как мой житейский сон,
Где яблони стоят в своём порядке
И муравьи свой строят Вавилон.
Сокрыт ромашкой телефонный кабель
И муравьиный Вавилон сокрыт...
Ещё мне снится, что воскреснет Авель
И Каина ревнивого простит.

[1992]

This mystery's not enigmatic…

This mystery's not enigmatic,
But simple, like my daily dream:
Apple-trees standing there, obedient,
While ants construct their Babylon.
With camomile the telephone cable
Is coated, as is the ants' Babylon.
Again I dream of the resurrection of Abel
Who has forgiven envious Cain.

[1992]

Сетчатка глазная…

Сетчатка глазная
Сильней браконьерских сетей, –
И птица лесная,
И рыба речная
Легко умещаются в ней,

Но не погибают,
А крыльями и чешуёй
Сей мир отражают,
В котором блуждает
И взор вопросительный твой.

Мой отрок чудесный,
Мой честолюбивый мудрец!
Скажу тебе честно:
И мне не известно,
Кто дичь на земле, кто – ловец.

[1991]

52

The retina holds…

The retina holds
More than the poacher's net.
The bird in the woods,
And fish in the stream
Find room in it.

But they do not perish.
Feather and scale
Reflect the world
In which as well
Wanders your curious gaze.

My wonderful lad,
My luminary,
I don't know either,
Who here is the hunter
And who the quarry.

[1991]

Бегу на смерть, как зверь на ловца...

Бегу на смерть, как зверь на ловца,
И в этом есть моя хитреца –
Я смерть отвожу от того лица,
Которое берегу.

Мой бег навстречу смущает смерть,
И смерть в свою попадает сеть,
И значит, жить мне ещё и петь
На истринском берегу,

Где вязы старые нянчат птиц,
Где май выходит из всех границ –
Из всех зарниц, изо всех темниц.
А я на ловца бегу.

[1991]

I hasten towards death...

I hasten towards death,
Like hunted towards hunter.
And therein my cunning, deflecting death
From the one I guard.

My reckless course confuses death,
Which falls into its own trap.
And that means I'll live a little more to sing
On the Istria's banks,

Where ancient elms shelter their birds,
Where May oversteps all bounds –
From lightning flashes and dark spots.
I am hurrying towards the hunter.

[1991]

Я это всё, как в школе, проходила…

Я это всё, как в школе, проходила
В зыбучем сне, не склонная ко сну,
И старость так на детство походила,
Как осень поздняя на раннюю весну.

То ль гроб качался в небе, то ли зыбка...
Черна, как ночь, и словно день, светла,
То ль дьявола, то ль ангела улыбка,
Морщинясь в озере, по зеркалу плыла.

Но где же ты в текущем дне, в насущном
Хрестоматийном хлебе бытия?
А я давным-давно живу в грядущем,
Как в римском кодексе забытая статья.

[1991]

I went through all this, as in school...

I went through all this, as in school
In troubled sleep and not disposed to dream,
And old age has resembled childhood,
As late autumn does early spring.

It was a coffin or a cradle
Rocked in the night sky or by day.
The devil's smile or an angel's
Puckering, floats in the mirror of the lake.

But where are you today,
In the daily bread, life's textbook?
Long have I been living in the future,
Like a forgotten article in a Roman codex.

[1991]

Погибель крáдется, как хитрая воровка

Погибель крáдется, как хитрая воровка.
Московский загород. Мороз и тишина.
Сияет Сириус, как синяя спиртовка,
Когда спиртовка зажжена.

И в стройном космосе свои, наверно, страхи.
При этой тихости навряд ли я усну.
Но ямб навязчивый и робкий амфибрахий
Со мной разделят тишину.

И одиночество, и ужас им доверю,
Разлад, сумятицу, российскую тщету,
Опять подобную затравленному зверю,
Стремящемуся в темноту.

Всегда голодная, холодная воровка,
Смерть тихой сапою ступает по земле –
На амфибрахии затянута верёвка,
И ямб качается в петле.

Но кто я, собственно, – кликуша иль шутиха?
Откуда Сириус, оттуда и петля.
Всё образуется – потрескивает тихо
И звёздный спирт, и снежная земля.

[1993]

Disaster, stealthy as a thief

Disaster, stealthy as a thief.
A Moscow suburb. Frost and quiet.
Sirius shines, like a spirit-lamp,
Bluely, when the oil's been lit.

Even the lucid cosmos has its fears.
In this quiet, I'll not fall asleep.
The obtrusive iamb and meek amphibrach
Will share the silence with me.

And I'll entrust to them my solitude and fear,
Discord, confusion, Russian vanity,
Which is like a hunted animal,
Streaming away into the dark.

Always the cold and famished thief,
Death slyly treads the earthly ways –
The cord is tightened on the amphibrach
And the iamb swings in a noose.

Who am I then – hysteric, joker?
Hence Sirius, as too the noose.
All will be well – the snowy earth
Is crackling, and the starry fuel.

[1993]

Клён кадит, и клочьями червонными…

Клён кадит, и клочьями червонными
Сладкий дым над свалкою плывёт,
Осень над отбросами зловонными
Службу служит, и душа поёт.

Жизнь прошла у жизни на обочине.
Горюшка немало претерпев,
Стал острее глаз, а слух отточенной,
И отзывчивее каждый нерв.

Шевелятся волосы на темени
То ли у меня, то ль у земли:
Многие живые стали тенями,
Ожили, которые ушли.

[1994]

В несчастных я себя не числю…

В несчастных я себя не числю,
Мне по сердцу моё житьё
В дремучей пропасти меж мыслью
И воплощением её.

Не это ль русская повадка –
Себя блаженно истязать,
Смеяться горько, плакать сладко
И на соломинке плясать.

[1994]

The maple's incense, crimson rags...

The maple's incense, crimson rags
Of sweet mist above the rubbish dump,
Autumn by the stinking garbage
Does its duty, and the soul gives voice.

By the roadside, life passed life by,
Enduring a panoply of grief,
The hearing more keen, sharper the eye,
And each nerve-end more responsive.

The hair stands on the back of the head,
The earth's or mine:
Many of the living are now shades;
Those who have left are reborn.

[1994]

I don't consider myself one of the unfortunate...

I don't consider myself one of the unfortunate,
My life suits me well
In the somnolent gulf between thought
And its embodiment.

Isn't it, though, the Russian way
To torture oneself ecstatically,
To laugh bitterly, to weep sweetly
And to dance upon a straw?

[1994]

61

Такая мгла...

Такая мгла,
Что тень светла
На фоне тьмы.
И я жила и не могла
Просить взаймы
Ни хлеба-соли, ни рубля
И ни тепла.
Но где же небо, где земля?
Такая мгла,
Что я свечусь, словно мишень,
И я кричу:
Убей меня, я – только тень,
Я спать хочу.

[1995]

Such darkness...

Such darkness,
The shadow is bright
Against the dark.
I was never able to ask
For hospitality, still less a loan,
Or human warmth.
But where's the sky, the earth?
Such darkness,
I stand out, like a target;
I scream:
Kill me, I'm just a shade!
I want to sleep!

[1995]

В жизни многошумной…

В жизни многошумной,
Где царит число,
Быть хотела умной,
Да не повезло.

В бытности короткой,
Где надменно зло,
Быть хотела кроткой,
Да не повезло.

В памяти столь дробной
Что произошло?
Быть хотела доброй,
Да не повезло.

В сфере разобщённой
Звёздное табло...
Быть бы мне прощённой,
Да не повезло.

[1996]

In a vociferous life…

In a vociferous life
Where numbers count,
I want to be clever
But just can't.

In a short life
Where evils prance,
I want to be meek
But just can't.

In my disrupted memory,
What happened?
I want to be kind
But just can't.

In this alien sphere
Is a scoreboard of stars.
I should have been forgiven –
Not a chance!

[1996]

Помню я сны Авраама и Сарры…

Помню я сны Авраама и Сарры,
Вопли Ионы в кипящей волне.
…Нет, не желаю писать мемуары,
Это занятие не по мне.

Воспоминания – для беззаветно
Ищущих в смерти свои следы.
Память есть то, что тебе незаметно,
Как организму процент воды.

[1997]

Господи, дай ему силы…

Господи, дай ему силы
Встретить и эту весну,
Где голосистые пилы
Трогают ель и сосну,

Где низвергаются пылко
Снежные глыбы с домов
Под золотистой развилкой
То ль облаков, то ль веков.

Господи, сделай благое,
Дай ему в лето окно
И горьковато-сухое
Белой берёзы вино.

I remember Abraham's dream and Sarah's...

I remember Abraham's dream and Sarah's,
In the seething waters, Jonah's scream...
No, I've no desire to write my memoirs,
That's not a job for the likes of me.

Reminiscences are for those who selflessly seek
Traces of self in mortality.
Memory is what is imperceptible,
As its water content is to the body.

[1997]

Lord, give him the strength...

Lord, give him the strength
To see in this spring too,
With its loud-voiced saws
Tipping pine and spruce,

With its blocks of snow
Rumbling down from the eaves,
Under the golden prod
Of clouds or years.

And, Lord, one more good deed –
Give him a berth
By a window with a summer view,
And the dry wine of the birch.

[2000]

67

Мы, русские, на мифы падки…

Мы, русские, на мифы падки.
Хоть землю ешь, хоть спирт глуши,
Мы все заложники загадки
Своей же собственной души.

Змею истории голубим,
Но, как словами ни криви.
Себя до ненависти любим
И ненавидим до любви.

Заздравные вздымая чаши,
Клянём извечную судьбу, –
Болит избранничество наше,
Как свежее клеймо на лбу.

[2000]

Myth has us Russians in thrall…

Myth has us Russians in thrall,
Whether down on our luck or high.
We are all hostages to our soul,
That wondrous entity.

We stroke the snake of history,
But however you bend our words,
We love ourselves to the point of loathing
And loathe ourselves to the point of love.

Raising our cups in a general toast,
We curse our everlasting fate for now –
What has been allotted hurts,
Like a fresh brand mark on the brow.

[2000]

Всё, что мной пережито, – рассказано

Марине Красиной

Всё, что мной пережито, – рассказано.
Слезы – это не бисер метать.
И, людскою насмешкой наказана,
Я в глухую ушла благодать.

Хуже нет быть до донышка понятой
Или выплаканной до конца,
И в траву с головою приподнятой
Я спускаюсь с гнилого крыльца.

Пробираясь крапивными дебрями,
Подхожу к одинокой сосне.
Ничего я не знаю о дереве,
И оно – ничего обо мне.

[2000]

Everything I have lived through has been told
To Marina Krasina

Everything I have lived through has been told.
Tears are not pearls to be cast.
And, subject to human mockery,
I withdrew to my blissful backwoods.

Nothing's worse than to be understood in depth,
Or sobbed for till there are no more tears,
With head raised high, I step
From the rickety porch into the grass.

Making my way through nettle-thickets,
I come to a solitary pine tree.
I know nothing about it
And it knows nothing about me.

[2000]

В саду что ни день, то новинка

В саду что ни день, то новинка.
Шиповник проснулся чуть свет,
И розочка, как балеринка,
Отважилась на пируэт.

И глупо и несправедливо,
Что, новости сада любя,
Я чувствую так сиротливо
И так одиноко себя.

Я вижу сквозь вспышки восторга,
Не знающего забытья,
Как время выносит из морга
Отснившийся сон бытия.

[2000]

Every morning, there's something new

Every morning, there's something new.
The dog-rose wakes at break of day,
And the rosebud, ballerina-like,
Is trying out a pirouette.

And it is foolish and unfair
That, so drawn to what is new,
I should feel utterly alone
And orphaned there.

I see, in my shock –
It cannot be dismissed –
Time bearing from the morgue
The extinct dream: I exist.

[2000]

Свистульки, трещотки, звонки,
гребешки, кастаньеты...

Свистульки, трещотки, звонки, гребешки, кастаньеты –
Какое в лесу вавилонское разноязычье!
К Создателю птичьи молитвы и гнёзда воздеты,
Отсюда, наверное, все привилегии птичьи.

А что небородные думают о земнородных, –
Не хватит фантазии мне, а тем более знанья.
А птицам известно ль, что несколько точек исходных
Мы взяли у них для старательного подражанья?

Так музыка создана, так создаются поныне
С Икаровых дней все летательные аппараты.
Но прежде – Господни крылатые стражи в пустыне,
И на Арарате – ковчега разведчик крылатый.

Целительна музыка. Флейты, виолы и лютни
Меня примиряют и с тем, что крылаты ракеты.
И я забываю, что дни моей родины люты,
Заслышав свистульки, звонки, гребешки, кастаньеты.

[2000]

74

Rattles, bells, combs, castanets...

Rattles, bells, combs, castanets –
A veritable Babel in the woods!
Addressed to the Creator, bird-prayers, nets,
Hence, all bird privileges, no doubt.

And what do the unbearded think of the earth-born –
I'm short of fantasies, and still more of knowledge.
But do the birds know what we have taken from them,
Copying, as we did, their several promising starts.

That's how music came about, and from Icarus
To now, all flying machines.
Before, it was the winged guards of the Lord in the wilderness,
And on Ararat the Ark's winged scout.

Music heals. Flutes, viols, lutes
Reconcile me even to the fins of rockets.
And I forget that my motherland's days were cruel,
Listening to rattles, bells, combs, castanets.

[2000]

Ворона

Ветер качает деревьев верхи,
И на берёзе ворона
Громко, в раскачку слагает стихи:
Родина, крона, корона!

Царственно мнится ей: это она
Так раскачала берёзу,
Что междождливая голубизна
Дарит ей жёлтую розу.

Кажется: держит на чёрном крыле
Розу осеннего солнца,
Кажется: всё на огромной земле
Царством вороньим зовётся.

Я в междождливое небо смотрю,
Вижу всё то, что не снится,
И верноподданно благодарю
Дерево, ветер и птицу.

[2000]

Crow

The wind sways the tree-tops,
And on a birch tree a crow out loud
Composes poetry, as he rocks:
Homeland, crowland, crown...

Regally he thinks it's he who
Has moved the birch tree so
That between showers, the blue
Might offer it a yellow rose.

That in his black wings he enfolds
The rose of the autumn sun,
That everything on this vast earth
Belongs to the Crow kingdom.

And, between showers, I gaze
Skywards, see the unheard,
The undreamed, and loyally
Thank tree, wind, and bird.

[2000]

Я замечала: в счастье ли, в печали …

Я замечала: в счастье ли, в печали, –
Все от меня ужасно уставали.

И лес устал от странности моей
Любить людей и избегать людей.

А от моих мятущихся историй
Когда-то уставало даже море.

Устали от меня и небеса
И ленятся закрыть мои глаза.

И может быть, когда меня не станет,
Моя могила от меня устанет.

[2000]

Тихие дни и тихие вечера

Тихие дни и тихие вечера.
А в телевизоре – взрывы, убийства, война.

Тихие дни и тихие вечера.
А в Интернете – безумные письмена.

Тихие дни и тихие вечера.
А в телефоне – тревожные голоса.

Тихие дни и тихие вечера, –
Плюнь мне в глаза и отвечу: божья роса.

[2001]

I noticed, everybody got...

I noticed, everybody got
Tired of me, happy or not.

The woods tired of my curious ways:
Keeping a distance even as I drew close.

And of my shifting tales, the sea
As well at one time wearied of me.

The cloudbank in the sky also tires
And is loath to close my eyes.

And, perhaps, when I am through,
My grave will weary of me too.

[2000]

Quiet days and quiet evenings

Quiet days and quiet evenings.
But on the box: killings, blasts.

Quiet days and quiet evenings.
But on the Net: endless prattle.

Quiet days and quiet evenings.
But over the phone: anxious voices.

Quiet days and quiet evenings,
Spit in my face, I'll murmur: God's dew!

[2001]

Музыка

Сижу на диете, но вместо меня
Вдоволь и ест и пьёт
Дикая музыка зимнего дня
И торфяных болот.

О как необуздан её аппетит –
Такую не взять на бал,
То, как кикимора, заверещит,
То разобьёт бокал,

И служат капли вина и стекла
Свистулькой её губам.
И высоковольтную ноту взяла, –
Сосулькой – по проводам, –

И свет отрубила, и так хрустит
Орехом и сухарём,
Что слышно, как наст на болоте трещит
И ухает в сердце моём.

[2002]

Music

I'm on a diet, but in my stead
The wild music of the peat
And of the winter's day
Drinks and eats.

How unbridled is its appetite –
You can't take this one to the ball,
Now it lets out a goblin squeal,
And now it is smashing a bowl.

It is served a brew of wine and shards,
Like a tin whistle to the lips.
And emits a high-voltage shriek,
Like an icicle down the line.

And it's cut out the light and is crunching
Like nuts or hardened bread,
Audible as the ice crust giving.
A cry resounds in my head.

[2002]

Размотала судьба предо мной моток...

Размотала судьба предо мной моток
Узловатых лесных дорог,
Доломаю я здесь мой век!
Одинок-в людской толпе человек,
А в толпе деревьев не одинок.

Меж деревьями я не хожу бочком,
Не верчусь волчком, не лежу ничком,
Как валежник или вода.
Спой мне, птичка с красным воротничком,
О строительстве своего гнезда.

Над твоим зрачком хохолок торчком...
Ах пичуга с красным воротничком,
Улетают и от тебя птенцы,
Разлетаются кто куда.
А от крылышек в воздухе нет следа, –
Только горлышек бубенцы, бубенцы...

[2002]

Destiny unwound its skein…

Destiny unwound its skein
Of knotted forest paths.
Here I live out my life!
Alone, in the human crowd,
But in the crowd of trees not alone.

I do not nudge my way among the trees,
Do not contort myself like a wolf,
Or lie prone, like wind-fallen branches or water.
Sing to me, red-ruffed bird
About how you built your nest.

A crest stands above those eyes…
Ah, bird with a red ruff,
Your fledglings flee as well,
They fly all over the place.
And their wings leave not a trace,
Only the bells of their narrow throats, the bells.

[2002]

Ода голосу

Белле Ахмадулиной

Этому голосу быть не может износу, –
Он соткан из пуха и выдоха летних деревьев,
Из облачных водорослей, из океанского ворса,
Из галактических нитей и ангельских перьев.

Однако и прост, как уличное просторечье,
Как над семью холмами летучее колоколье,
И лишь для его обладателя он не легче
Камня, который в пустыне вопит от боли,

Когда терновник прожилки когтит, а в сердце
Втекает закланной овцы кипящее сало.
Но это известно камню и словопевцу,
А голос выглядит так, как я его описала.

[2002]

Душа охладелое тело...

Душа охладелое тело
Покинет оторопело
И станет началом начал, –
Сияньем, которое пело,
И звуком, который сиял.

[2002]

Ode to a Voice
To Bella Akhmadulina

This voice will stand any amount of wear –
It is made from down and the summer trees' breath,
Cloudy algae, oceanic pile,
Galactic threads and angels' feathers.

But it is simple, too, like street talk,
Like floating bells over the seven hills,
And only for its owner is it not lighter
Than a stone in the wilderness, exclaiming in pain,

When the vein's thorn claws, and into the heart
Drips the burning fat of the sacrificial lamb.
But this is well-known to stone and singer of songs,
With the voice just as I described.

[2002]

Dumbfounded, the spirit...

Dumbfounded, the spirit
Will forsake its indifferent host
And become the common ground –
A sounding glow,
And a glowing sound.

[2002]

После жизни прошу меня не сжигать…

После жизни прошу меня не сжигать –
Пусть насытится червь, насладится малинник.
После жизни не стану я вспоминать
Ни сиротских лет, ни душевных клиник.

После жизни сама с собой помирюсь
И увижу всю музыку в ре-мажоре, –
И тебя, сироту приютившая Русь,
И тебя, моя зыбка – азийское море.

Нет малины на кладбище там, где родня,
Ну а здесь песчаного нет покрывала.
После смерти? – Но это не про меня,
А про ту, что ни разу не умирала.

[2001]

Do not cremate me after life...

Do not cremate me after life –
Let the worm have its fill, the raspberry-canes enjoy.
After life, I'll not recall
Either orphanage or psychiatric clinic.

After life, I shall come to terms with myself
And all music will be in the major key –
And Russia, sheltering the orphan,
And you, my cradle, asian sea.

There are no raspberries in the graveyard, only
My dear ones. No sandy pall.
After death? It's not about me,
But the one who did not die at all.

[2001]

Мгновенное

Навеки меня просквозила
Мгновенного солнца стрела.
Что есть, то и есть. А что было –
Лишь тень от весла и крыла.

Мне всякое лишнее знанье –
Как пух с подзаборной травы.
Мне нравится ветра дыханье
И чуждо дыханье молвы.

Лишь ветер мне радость внушает,
Как хлеб, что сейчас испечён.
Прошедшего ветер не знает
И будущим не удручён.

[2002]

Instantaneous

The arrow of the instantaneous sun
Has pierced me to the core.
What is,is; as for what was –
Only the shadow of a wing, an oar.

Any superfluous knowledge for me is
Like fluff from under the gate.
The wind pleases me
And alien is rumour's breath.

Only the wind brings happiness,
Like the smell of freshly baked bread.
The wind does not know what has happened,
And is not dismayed by what's ahead.

[2002]

Вдали от Содома

Я выдохнула память. И для вдоха
Теперь нужна мне новая эпоха
Или хотя бы – новое окно
В иной пейзаж, где лавр дорогу славит,
Где солнце заходящее оставит
На мне своё родимое пятно.

Оно похоже на почтовый штемпель
Да и на пломбу на вагоне «мебель»,
И на тавро, которым метят скот, –
Хочу быть кем угодно, чем угодно,
Но лишь бы с мёртвой точки безысходной
Мне сдвинуться и высмотреть исход.

А он, наверно, там, где был вначале,
Где позже мирру с тёрном повенчали.
На кой мне ляд, однако, та страна,
Иль град, где пощадили только Лота?
Мне выйти всего-навсего охота
За крестовину этого окна!

[2001]

Far from Sodom

I breathe out memory. To breathe it in
For now, a new epoch is needed,
Or a new window may suffice –
With a different aspect, laurelled roads,
Where the setting sun deposits
Its birth-mark on me.

This is like a postage stamp or the word
"Furniture" on the side of a van
And the brand-mark on cattle, –
I'd like to be whoever, whatever,
If only to move from the dead point, dead-end
And find the exit therefrom.

But probably it's where it first was,
Where later they crowned thorns with myrrh,
That country, I don't know it now,
Or city, where Lot alone was spared?
All in all I must transcend
The intersecting lines of this window!

[2001]

В лесу

У тебя в глазах вековечный растаял лёд,
У меня в глазах вековая застыла темь,
По-научному мы как будто – с катодом анод,
По-народному мы – неразлучны, как свет и тень.

Я – жена твоя и припадаю к твоим стопам,
Увлажняю слезами и сукровицей ребра,
Из которого вышла, а ты, мой свет, мой Адам,
Осушаешь мой лоб, ибо почва в лесу сыра.

Много тысячелетий прошло с тех эдемских пор,
Лишь любовь не прошла, потому что одна она
Суть пространства и времени. А троянский раздор
И война, как и ныне, – из-за золотого руна.

Прежде – шерсть золотая, теперь – золотой песок…
Ради красного слова любовь называли певцы
Всех несчастий причиной (любовь возвышает и слог),
Но от лжи и у римской волчицы отсохли сосцы.

И певцы – ни при чём. За словцо я цепляюсь сама,
Как сейчас уцепилась за клюквенные персты…
Ах, мой свет, твоя тень не умрёт от большого ума,
А беззвучно исчезнет, как только исчезнешь ты.

[2001]

In the Woods

In your eyes the permafrost has melted;
In my eyes the permadark has set.
Scientifically, like anode and cathode;
More ordinarily, inseparable, light and shade.

Trailing behind, I falter – wife I am,
Moistening you with my tears and the rib's lymph –
The rib whence I am sprung – my light, my Adam,
You mop my brow, for the forest floor is damp.

Since those Edenic times, millennia have passed;
Love has not, the very nub of space
And time. And the Trojan conflict,
As then, the *casus belli*, Golden Fleece.

Before it was the Fleece, now gold itself...
For effect, the singers have ascribed to love
All our misfortunes (love ennobles style as well),
But this lie makes the Roman she-wolf's milk dry up.

And the singers aren't to blame. I too grasp the word,
And now the cranberry-livid fingers grip tight...
Your shade will not die of too nimble a mind,
But be gone as soon as you're out, my light.

[2001]

93

У Яффских ворот

Я – твоя Суламифь, мой старый царь Соломон,
Твои мышцы ослабли, но твой проницателен взгляд.
Тайны нет для тебя, но, взглянув на зелёный склон,
Ты меня не узнаешь, одетую в платье до пят,
Меж старух, собирающих розовый виноград.

И раздев, не узнал бы: как волны песка мой живот,
И давно мои ноги утратили гибкость лоз,
Грудь моя, как на древней пальме увядший плод,
А сквозь кожу сосуды видны, как сквозь крылья стрекоз.
Иногда я тебя поджидаю у Яффских ворот.

Но к тебе не приближусь. Зачем огорчать царя?
Славен духом мужчина, а женщина – красотой.
От объятий твоих остывая и вновь горя,
Наслаждалась я песней не меньше, чем плотью тугой,
Ведь любовь появилась Песне благодаря.

Ах, какими словами ты возбуждал мой слух,
Даже волос мой сравнивал с солнечным завитком...
Для бездушной страсти сгодился бы и пастух.
Но ведь дело не в том, чтоб бурлила кровь кипятком,
А чтоб сердце взлетало, как с персиков спелый пух.

Я вкушала слова твои, словно пчела пыльцу,
Неужели, мой царь, твой любовный гимн красоте,
До тебя недоступный ни одному певцу,
Только стал ты стареть, привёл тебя к суете –
К поклоненью заморскому золотому тельцу?

В стороне от тебя за тебя всей любовью моей
Постоянно молюсь. И сейчас в тишине ночной
Зажигаю в песчаной посудине семь свечей,
Раздираю рубаху и сыплю пепел печной
На седины: Царя укрепи, а тельца забей!

[2001]

At the Jaffa Gate

I'm your Shulamith, my old King Solomon,
Your muscles are slack, but your sight still sharp.
Nothing's withheld from you, but peering at the slope,
You do not recognize me, draped from head to foot,
Among the old women gathering grapes.

And were I naked, you'd not know me, my belly
Like undulant sands, legs stiff, unlike the vine,
My breast, the withered fruit of an ancient palm,
And the veins showing, as in a dragon-fly's wings.
Sometimes I wait for you at the Jaffa Gate.

But I do not approach. Why distress the king?
A man's renowned for valour, a woman for her skin.
Cooling after your embrace and once again on fire,
I delighted in song no less than in flesh.
It was the song made love reveal itself.

Ah, those words with which you compared
My hair to the flashing sunlight.
For a soulless love any dull shepherd will do.
But the point is not to make the blood boil,
Or even the heart lift, like down off peach blossom.

I inhaled your speech, as a bee inhales pollen,
My king, Solomon, your love-hymn to beauty,
Unprecedented, no singer before…
Only you grew old, and with this came vanity –
And prostration before the golden calf?

I turn aside and pray for you still
With all my love. And now,
In the quiet of evening, I light seven candles
In a sandy vessel, as I rend my shift,
And strew your grey hair with grains of ash:
May the King grow strong and the calf be slain!

[2001]

Ревность

В уходящую спину смущенно смотрю из окна...
Твоя ревность и трогательна и смешна.
Неужели не видишь, что я и стара и страшна,
И помимо тебя никому на земле не нужна?

Ну какая тут трогательность и какой тут смех?
Ты от нашего крова, одетого в мшистый мех,
И от быта, сплошь состоящего из прорех,
Так и рвёшься, ревнуя, отвадить буквально всех.

А приходят к нам исключительно из доброты –
С крыши мох соскрести, кое-где подвинтить винты,
Да ещё приносят мне молодые цветы
В благодарность, что жив и мной обихожен ты.

А ещё и тайная есть корысть у гостей,
А вернее, мечта – до старых дожить костей
И любимыми быть, и на склоне преклонных дней
Слушать гимны себе, что свежей любых новостей.

И ревнуют меня к тебе как любви пример,
Так что ты свою ревность бездумную поумерь,
Чтобы в мире, где столько зла и безумных потерь,
Всяк входящему я открывала с улыбкою дверь.

[2001]

Jealousy

I look out the window at the retreating back.
Your jealousy is both touching and comical.
Can't you see I am old and scary, a witch,
And apart from you no-one needs me at all!

Well, what's so touching and funny in that?
Jealous, you're keen to send all of them packing
Away from our home, with its roof's mossy coat,
And our life, which consists entirely of sacking!

But they do not desist, out of kindness of sorts –
From scraping away the moss, checking a rafter,
And they bring flowers as well, to thank me
For your still being alive and so well looked after.

And they steal away with something else, a notion
Of how to survive as the years advance
And still be loved, and, with time running out,
To listen to eulogies, fresher than the news.

And my attachment, the truth of my love, no less,
They envy. So, keep your jealousy buttoned up!
In this world, with its surfeit of painful loss,
Let me open the door with a smile on my lips.

[2001]

Наша встреча

Дятел долбит по коре, – легко ль червяка добыть?
Я поднялась на заре и медлю тебя будить.
Своё ты отвоевал – у каждого свой мороз:
Ты ладожский лёд целовал и по волжскому полз.
А в морге был мой мороз: пошла сирота в санчасть
Тянуть погребальный воз, чтоб с голоду не пропасть.
Есть сокровенный смысл в стыковке судьбы с судьбой, –
Чтоб разморозить жизнь, встретились мы с тобой.

[2001]

Отцвели облака

Отцвели облака. Осыпаются крупным дождём.
Мы с тобой не века, мы с тобой только дождь переждём.
Как похож на кольчугу твой плащ! Под широким плащом
Мы с тобой не разлуку, а дождь проливной подождём.
Под твоим макинтошем до дрожи плечу горячо.
Ты уйдёшь, мой хороший, и стану я гладить плечо
Это, левое, что примостилось к плечу твоему.
Ты уйдёшь. Вспыхнет дождь, прикоснувшись к лицу моему.

[Из журнала «Арион», 3-2003]

Our meeting

The woodpecker chips at the bark – easy route to the worm?
I take my time waking you, though I rose at dawn.
Your war is over – to each his own frost.
You skated on the Volga, iced Ladoga kissed,
But my frost was the morgue: from orphan to orderly,
So as not to starve, I pulled funeral trolleys.
There's a sacred meaning in this meeting of fate and fate –
It was to unfreeze life that you and I met.

[2001]

The clouds have lost their bloom

The clouds have lost their bloom. A downpour descends.
You and I wait, not for ever, just till the rain stops.
How like a shirt of mail is your raincoat! Under it,
You and I wait, not before parting, but for the pelting rain to stop
Under your mackintosh, my shoulder is so warm it trembles.
You will leave, my love, and I shall stroke the shoulder.
This one, the left, that was touching yours.
You will leave, and again the rain will brush my face.

[from *Arion*, No. 39, 3-2003]

Смотрю я с горы, к тому же с четвёртого этажа

Смотрю я с горы, к тому же с четвёртого этажа.
Пустыня, как в море, вливается в окоём,
Шатры бедуинов, что паруса на нём,
Небо слоится, пеной морской дрожа.
Когда-то сюда мы приезжали вдвоём.

Солнце садилось – резко очерченный белый круг
Нам предвещал жёлтой луны восход –
Солнце с луною не ведает здесь разлук.
Но нет тебя больше со мною, и вот
Душа моя делает тысячемильный крюк

В снег подмосковный, где ты на вечные веки увяз,
Посох отбросив, чтобы служил он мне
Компасной стрелкой. Исполнила я указ:
Скоро как месяц в библейской гощу стороне,
Не отводя от песков запоминающих глаз.

Гроздьями с пальмы свисают финиковые огни,
Чешет об иглы алоэ свой бок эвкалипт.
Глас, вопиющий в пустыне в текущие дни,
Очень похож на скрипучий московский лифт,
Где целовались, когда подымались одни.

Трудно мне дался на гору подъём, тем паче четвёртый этаж.
В небо пустыня идёт, и верблюжий горб
Не отличим от облака. В этот пейзаж
Будто машина в гараж въезжает сосновый гроб.
Смерть твоя – это явь. Жизнь моя – это мираж.

[8 ноября 2003]

I look down from the mountain, the fourth floor

I look down from the mountain, the fourth floor.
A desert floods the vista, like a sea.
Tents of the Bedouin, like sails upon it.
The sky stratifies, trembling like foam.
At one time, we two were here together.

The sun set – a white outline foretold,
The ascension of the yellow moon –
The sun here never parts completely with the moon.
But you are no longer with me, and now
My soul makes a thousand-mile detour

Via the Moscow snows, where you stalled for good,
Discarding your staff, so it would serve
As a compass needle. I did as told:
Almost a month, a visitor, I remember,
In the Biblical land, my gaze fixed on the sands.

Like flames, bunches of dates from the palm-trees.
The eucalyptus scrapes the aloe's thorns.
The voice, crying now in the wilderness,
Is like the creaking Moscow elevator
We went in alone, and kissed.

The climb was hard to the fourth floor.
The wilderness continues upward, and the camel's hump
Can't be told apart from a cloud. This scape
Receives the pine coffin, as a car slides into a garage.
Your death is the reality; my life a mirage.

Обнажённые мысли живут без прикрас

Обнажённые мысли живут без прикрас.
Поговорка врёт человеку,
Дескать, дважды нельзя... Но в тысячный раз
Я вхожу в ту же самую реку.

Те же серые камни вижу на дне,
Красен тот же карась плавниками,
То же самое солнце в синем пятне
Моет жёлтые пятна веками.

В ту же реку раките рыдать не лень,
Те же воды рябят напевно,
В ту же самую реку вхожу что ни день,
В ту же самую жизнь ежедневно.

[7 ноября 2003]

Naked thoughts live unembellished

Naked thoughts live unembellished.
That saying's a lie, you can't
Twice and so forth, whatever it is.
A thousandth time I enter the same river.

And I see the same grey stones on the bottom,
The same carp with its gristly fins,
The same sun in the blue patch of sky
Washes the yellow spots for ages.

In the same river the willow weeps,
The same waters ripple tunefully,
No day passes but into the same river
I enter, the very same life.

[7 November 2003]

Biographical Notes

INNA LISNIANSKAYA was born in Baku in 1928. Her first publication was in 1948 and her first poetry collection appeared in 1957. From 1979, for many years, her books appeared only abroad, including: *V priogorode Sodmoma* ['In the Suburb of Sodom'], 2002; *Veter pokoya* ['Wind of peace'], 1998; and *Posle vsego* ['After everything'], 1994. In recent years she has published several more collections in Russia and has contributed regularly to all major literary periodicals. Lisnianskaya was married to the late Semyon Lipkin, also a leading Russian poet, and her most recent collection consists partly of an elegy to him. She lives in Moscow.

DANIEL WEISSBORT edited the magazine *Modern Poetry in Translation* (1965-2004) and directed the Translation Workshop at the University of Iowa. His most recent collection is *Letters to Ted* (Anvil, 1998). His most recent anthology is *Contemporary Russian Women Poets*, co-edited with his wife Valentina Polukhina. He is Research Fellow at King's College, London, and Honorary Professor in the Centre for Translation & Comparative Cultural Studies, University of Warwick.

ELAINE FEINSTEIN is a prize-winning poet, novelist and biographer. She was made a Fellow of the Royal Society of Literature in 1980. In 1990, she received a Cholmondeley Award for Poetry, and was given an Honorary D.Litt from the University of Leicester. Her versions of the poems of Marina Tsvetaeva were first published in 1971, and remain in print from OUP / Carcanet in the UK and Penguin in USA. Her *Collected Poems and Translations* (2002) was a Poetry Book Society Special Commendation. Her biography of Anna Akhmatova, which she began writing in 1999, comes out in June 2005 from Weidenfeld and Nicholson.